College 101

College 101

101 Notes of Wisdom for College Students From College Students

Written and Compiled by
Benjamin Lye & Nicholas Dyer

COLLEGE 101

Copyright © 2008 by BN Publishing House
Indianapolis, IN.

Cover design by Benjamin Lye
Book design by Benjamin Lye

Printed in the United States of America

First Printing: December 2008

ISBN 978-0-578-00377-1

Acknowledgements

We would like to thank our editor, Bethany Lye. Without her discerning eye, this book would be totally incomprehensible. We would also like to thank our agent, Helen Zimmerman, and everyone who contributed ideas (especially Thomas Hopkins who was a constant source of knowledge).

Noticeably absent from this list is our parents, who cut-off our college funds after four years and forced us to graduate.

Contents

Introduction

If you are looking for a guide that outlines how to score a 4.0 G.P.A. in college, keep searching. "College 101" is not that type of book. In fact, we—the authors—are not quite Pulitzer prize-winning writers or professors with a string of distinguished abbreviations after our names. And to our credit, we will not tell you what all of the other books will tell you: That you should sit in the front row of every lecture hall, study three hours per hour of class time, sleep for eight hours each night and aim to graduate in four years or less.

Pretending that college is *just* about academics is ridiculous. And we certainly don't want to let you dive into higher education— and its great frat party of social learning—unprepared. So, for anyone curious about how to succeed in all facets of college life, including the dirty laundry, dating, drinking and—yes—studying aspects of that life, then this is the book for you.

And we should know. We graduated from an academically challenging liberal arts school with a combined G.P.A. of 3.1. But, we also walked off campus with an understanding that "the college experience" is about more than just your transcript or your last exam score. College is, in fact, about the friendships you form with the people around you and the life experiences that you have along the way. Lucky for you, we are here to make sure that you graduate from college without regretting a day. So, enjoy! You have just signed up for the best four years of your life!

Relationships 101

"A true friend is one who holds your hair while you puke."
- Madison Basch, Hanover College class of 2009

1. Tell Your Mom, "I Miss You."

These simple words will mean more to her than you can imagine.
Tell her often.

....

2. R.E.S.P.E.C.T.

Chances are, your girlfriend will not be impressed by loud belching, lewd jokes or beer chugging, in the same way your boyfriend probably won't want to carry that bright red purse around while you browse the One-Day Sale at Macy's. You do not have to change your personality when you're with your significant other, but DO aim to treat them with respect at all times—especially in group settings. Guys: stand up when your girlfriend walks into a room. Girls: Have some mercy on your boyfriend in front of his friends. It's probably not a good idea to blab about how he rubs on a pumpkin enzyme mask every Wednesday to try and clear up his acne. And the most important piece of advice any girl can take is to pay close attention to what a guy does, not what he says. Trust us.

....

3. Befriend Betty, The Chicken Nugget Woman

Make friends with the lunch ladies and learn the names of your housekeepers. Simple gestures such as giving him or her a holiday card or baking them cookies will go a very long way (and, in a perfect world, this will mean four years of extra chicken nuggets).

....

4. Graduate Without Baggage

The goal here is: Do not get pregnant or get anyone else pregnant. Do not catch an STD (or two or three). And whatever happens, DO NOT create a sex tape—it is guaranteed to resurface somewhere at the most inopportune time. In fact, as a general rule, do not videotape anything that you wouldn't want played at Christmas dinner—with your in-laws.

....

5. Phone Home

As you grow older, your parents will seem to grow smarter. The reality is that they were pretty damn smart all along. Call them often. They are an invaluable resource and, as you mature, your relationship with them will strengthen. By graduation, they will seem more like a friend than a parent.

....

6. Ask Permission & Be Informed

When you start dating a girl, and you're about to get intimate for the first time, ask permission for everything. You will win bonus points with her and keep yourself out of trouble.

When you first meet a guy, do not worry about impressing him. If he's approached you, then you have already made an impact. Instead, show him that you respect yourself and you're worth a good chase.

....

7. It's Not What You Know, It's Who You Know

This adage is especially true upon graduation, and it is never too early to make friends. Introduce yourself to as many people as possible. You will probably gain acceptance to graduate school or nail your first "real" job based on whom you know—not what you know.

....

8. Set The Mood

Create a make-out mix tape. Use it wisely. Keep it away from your friends and do not label it "Make-out Mix" on your computer.

....

9. Looks Aren't Everything

Contrary to what you may think, the cutest person in your Biology class may not be the greatest catch. Yes, she may be gorgeous and have an adorable British accent, but if she doesn't challenge you, you will get bored. And don't think that just because your prince charming is sporting a six-pack, he's the one. In 20 years, he could be all yours while working a minimum wage job and watching NASCAR all weekend. You deserve better. Shoot for someone who's attractive *with* personality and pay close attention to how they treat their mother. Still, have fun while it lasts.

....

10. Don't Date The Hottie Next Door

If they share a house with you, or if their dorm room is next to yours, don't date them. This may seem like a great idea at first kiss, but unless you are planning on getting serious—and losing all of your free time— avoid this scenario at all costs.

....

11. Create A Secret Code

Work out a "Do Not Enter" signal with your roommate. Be creative. Everyone knows what a tie on the doorknob means. A rubber band is less conspicuous, and it won't embarrass anyone. But, prepare for Plan B. The rubber band moment will probably arrive without warning, so talk to a good friend with a clean couch before your roommate has a chance to break out the secret signal.. Be sure to take your host out to breakfast the next morning (and it's ok to ask your roommate pay).

....

12. Everything You Need To Know To Play The College Dating Game

1) Girls love drama.

2) If you're a girl, guys are afraid of you. Be kind.

3) Every guy needs to be trained.

4) A relationship isn't official until it's Facebook official.

5) Guys: The standard mourning time after a breakup is one week per every six months of a relationship. On the other hand, girls will mourn one week for every month that a relationship lasted. This is an unspoken, undocumented law of love.

6) You must wait at least two weeks before attempting to date someone who has just ended another relationship.

7) If you spend the night with a girl four times in one week, you are dating.

8) Do not date a friend's ex unless you are ready to lose that friend.

9) If you end a relationship because you want to date someone else, you forfeit the right to ask for your belongings back (this is true even if you tell her a "gentler" excuse; be prepared to say bye-bye to your lucky T-shirt).

9.5) She knows the "gentler" excuse is not true.

....

13. Do Not Room With Your Best Friend

Roommates can become best friends. But, best friends generally make horrible roommates. This is especially true for females. In general, living with your best friend is a great way to lose them. Try moving down the hall from them, instead.

....

14. Remember Your Parents' Birthdays. They Remember Yours.

Schedule your family members' birthdays into your computer and be sure to send your mom and dad a card on their birthdays. That's right—send a real card. Do not send an E-card. Do not cop-out with a quick phone call. And before you start whining about shelling out $2.50 for a cheesy card, just remember: Your parents always remember your birthday and, chances are, their card contains money.

．．．．．．．．．．．．．．．．．．．．．．．．．．．．．．．．．．．．．．

15. Break Up With Your High-School Love

Trust us, this separation is inevitable. Just break off the relationship now so that you can enjoy college to the fullest.

....

Socializing 101

"Do it for the story."
- Ben Spain, Hanover College class of 2009

16. Hit The Road

Plan it, don't plan it, whatever—but break away for at least one real road trip every year. Packing five people, their beer and guitars into a Honda Civic is one of the surest ways to bond with your friends. But remember, the destination is not important—just make sure you have one!

....

17. You Will Not Remember The Nights When You Got Plenty Of Sleep

Instead, you will remember the nights where you randomly stayed up late with your friends talking about the meaning of life, watching your favorite movie and arguing about why snot is green. No matter what the clock says, if an opportunity arises to do something fun, do it. In college, sleep is optional.

....

18. A Taxi Fare Costs Less Than A D.U.I.

So you have to shell out $10 for a taxi—big deal. Your other options are parking ten miles away from the bar and then living in fear of a tow truck or scrambling to find a ride home at 4 am. Ten bucks is also better than hearing the disappointment in Mom's voice when you call her from jail after being arrested for a DUI. Besides, sometimes the cab ride turns out to be the best part of the night. So, stash a few bucks in your back pocket before you head out to party. You'll never regret it.

....

19. Do Not Pass Out With Your Shoes On

If you wake up in bed with your shoes on, you have passed out. This gives your friends free reign to "shame" you. Trust us—this is very bad news. So, kick off your shoes before calling it a night, and you will wake up the next morning without black Sharpie graffiti all over your face (or an embarrassing nickname to live down).

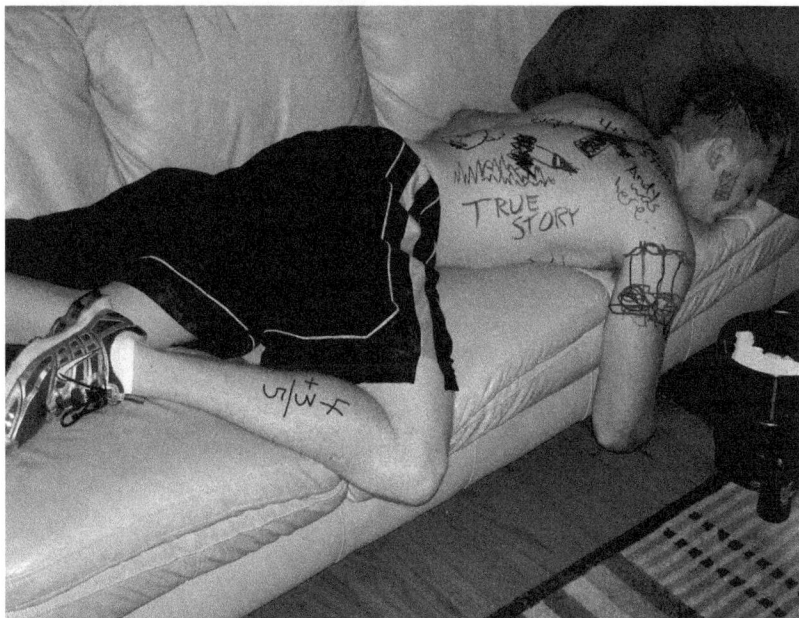

20. Learn To Dance

Dancing will be a fundamental part of your collegiate social life. If you can't dance, do not go to a party and stand against the wall. Practice alone in your room if you have to (NOT to your Make-out Mix Tape). Most important of all, don't tell anyone that you can't dance. Get out there and act like you know what you're doing. The great thing about dancing is that it's about confidence. If you act like you can dance, no one is going to tell you differently.

....

21. Play Hard To Get

Guys love women like girls love shoes. And just like women can't resist the season's latest "it" boots, guys will similarly obsess over their latest female fetish. Girls: Men will approach you and ask you out. Be prepared to say "No thanks" at any time. If he really likes you, he will try again.

....

22. Participate In At Least One Massive, Clever, Harmless Prank

This could mean having an impromptu water balloon fight, building a giant phallus out of snow or streaking across the quad in the middle of the night. Harmless pranks help relieve stress and make for great memories. Don't be afraid to get creative.

....

23. The Las Vegas Effect: Just Because You Can't Remember It, Doesn't Mean It Didn't Happen

*Note that this rule only applies if someone witnesses your act of stupidity. If there are no witnesses, and you cannot remember anything, nothing happened. If you spent all Friday night riding a plunger in your Sponge Bob underwear, be prepared for your friends to "refresh" your memory for the rest of your life. Apologize and laugh it off while burning any incriminating evidence. Chances are, the story will grow old sometime before you die.

....

24. Dress Sharp On The First Day Of Class. After That, No One Cares

On the first day of class, put some serious effort into your outfit—you'll impress your professors and classmates alike. If you're a girl, dress as if your teacher were your next door neighbor. Get attention for your smarts, not gratuitous skin shots. If you're a guy, pull out the iron and slap on a tie. But this day is the exception. For the rest of the school year, your personality—and not your clothes—will create the bigger impression. (For those lacking in the personality department, ignore this advice and keep dressing nicely for the rest of the year. Really.)

....

25. A Rx For Rough Mornings

The harder you party, the harder it is to wake up the next day. To make your post-party mornings run smoother, drink a glass of water and take two extra-strength Tylenol before heading to bed. The next morning, you may still slide out of bed, but you'll be ready for round two by nightfall.

....

26. You Can Keep Puking Long After You Think You're Finished

When you're a freshman, you may think you know your limits for drinking—but you don't. Drink responsibly and remember: You can puke long after you think you're finished. Do not—ever—sleep on your back after a long night of drinking or you will be in danger of choking on your puke in your sleep.

....

27. The Best Moments Are Rarely Planned

Planned events are fun, but spontaneous road trips, get-togethers and pranks contain an aura of excitement that can never be repeated. Enjoy as many of these moments as you can because they will turn out to be the best times of your life.

....

28. Join An Organization

College is full of opportunities, so try to do something new every year: painting, tennis lessons, the school newspaper. A special bonus for getting out of your comfort zone is that most people meet their boyfriend or girlfriend at social events (and not while sitting in front of the computer in a Halo 3 chat room). So, whatever grabs your interest, go for it. And it's ok to join a club just because cute twins are attending the meeting—especially if you want to find some "common-ground" to help get the spark started.

....

29. No One Wins In A Case Race

A case race is a daylong race to see who can be the first to drink an entire case of beer in 24 hours. Contrary to popular belief, no one wins a case race. Yes, everyone gets hammered. But if you lose, you're known for drinking like a nanny. If you win and actually manage to finish your case without puking: Congrats! You're fat and your liver just got its ass kicked.

....

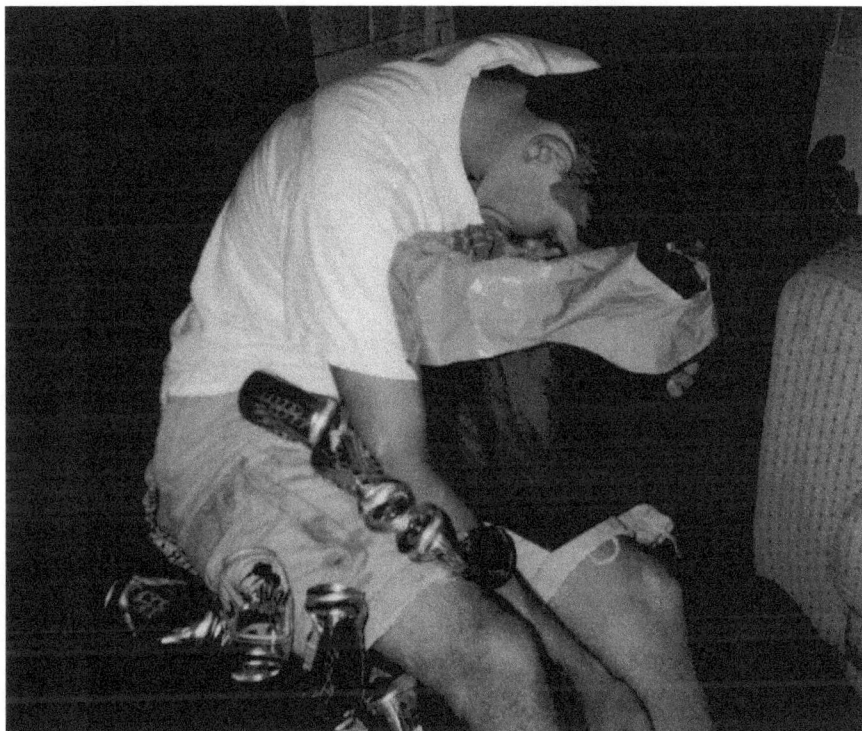

30. Any Game Can Be A Drinking Game

All drinking games have one crucial rule: you must drink. Try inventing your own drinking game. Play it all the time, with as many people as you can. Aim for immortalization. If you cannot think up a good game, just drink and call it a game. Like "1-2-3 drink." Believe us. This works.

....

31. Drink, But Don't Be A Drunk

People tend to love a drinker, but everyone feels sorry for the drunk (and just to set the record straight: alcohol is not a prerequisite for a good time. You can have plenty of fun sober, too). If you drink alone or without reason, you are a drunk. In both scenarios, hold off on the alcohol and self-reflect. Drink, but don't be a drunk and go out but not every night.

....

32. Halloween Is Fun Again

In high school, you were suddenly too "old" to dress up for Halloween. But in college, a Halloween costume is a must. If you don't know what to wear, collaborate. Group costumes always work well. If you do it right, you will spend a ridiculous amount of time plotting and creating your costume. It's all part of the fun.

....

33. The Things You Will Remember Most Are Probably The Things That Got You Into The Most Trouble

So take note: don't always follow the rules or do everything exactly as planned. Live a little. Luckily, your youth gives you a valid excuse to screw up. Milk your naiveté for all it's worth.

....

34. Develop Your Own Sense Of Style

Just make sure that your personal fashion statement does NOT involve:

1) Your high school letter jacket

2) Disney characters

3) A sleeveless muscle T-shirt

4) Socks with sandals

5) Chest hair (unless you are *extremely* cool)

6) Pajamas with holes (Pajamas without holes are fine for class)

Also: Velcro shoes are now cool. Embrace them.

....

35. Even If You Think You Are The Best Recreational Basketball Player That Ever Lived, You Are Not. You Probably Suck

Remember this when someone asks you to play in any type of intramural league. It is just intramurals. There is a reason you do not play for an actual team. The reason is: You suck.

....

36. 21st Birthdays = National Holidays

You will likely not make it to class the day after your 21st birthday. Don't kid yourself. And if your friend is turning 21, it is up to you to ensure that their birthday is an absolute blast. Arrive armed with a camera and ready to party (at milestones like this, where drunkenness may cloud the memories of everyone involved, photographic evidence is key. This way, the entire campus will know that you really did dance with a 75-year-old toothless grandpa at the bar).

....

37. Pour Your Own Drinks

Never drink from a cup that you did not pour for yourself. This way you know exactly what and how much is in what you are drinking. If you leave your cup sitting unattended at a party, consider it garbage and pour a new one. It only takes a second for someone to slip something in your drink.

....

38. Your Body Is Perfect

Ok, Ladies. For those of you who want a flatter stomach, bigger boobs or a better tan—stop it. Seriously. Guys dream about your body. They are oblivious to your self-professed anatomical flaws. You are their temple. What do men really notice? Confidence. A sense of style. A sense of humor (and if you're wearing one of those push-up Miracle Bras—no matter how near the start of the alphabet your breasts are—guys will notice this, too. And salivate). So, stop fretting about that mole on your shoulder or the size of your thighs. Enjoy what you've got. Embrace your body. All the men out there sure want to.

....

Academics 101

"Every time I learn something new, it pushes some old
stuff out of my brain."
-Homer Simpson

39. Don't Buy New Books. Ever.

Buying used textbooks will cut your school supply costs in half. Avoid new books at all costs and don't be afraid to forgo a hardcover issue for its money-saving soft-cover twin. If you buy online save on shipping by sticking to a single reputable website such as Amazon.com. A few words of caution, however: Read closely. Make sure that the title of the book you are looking to order matches, exactly, the title of the book required for your class. Secondly, don't wait—order the books as soon as you know you'll need them to ensure that you will be prepared for that first day of class.

Another way to save some money is to write to your professors during the summer and get a list of the required books and then on the first day you return to campus visit your local libraries. Speed is a necessity here as most of the books will not last past the first day.

Also, get more return on your investment by trying to sell your textbooks yourself, either online or directly to classmates and friends. Also, if your bookstore does not want your books back remember that there are lots of online stores that will buy older editions for cash.

....

40. If You Attend Every Class, You Will Not Flunk

You can absorb some of your teacher's lessons just by sitting—awake—in class. So, no matter how hungover or sick you are, get to class. If you go everyday, you will not fail. Your attendance also shows your teacher that you are taking their class seriously. Nothing frustrates professors more than students who scramble "to be a good student" only at the very end of a semester.

....

41. The Art Of Studying

Tip #1: Find a quiet place to study.

Tip #2: Keep your study place a secret—even from your friends.

(College is full of distractions. Sometimes, you will need to say "no" to cookouts and sorority parties and make your academic education the priority. When this time comes, turn off Instant Messenger and close your Internet browser. Pack snacks, charge your iPod and head to your secret study space. Do not emerge until you've memorized your material.)

....

42. Oftentimes, The Professor Is More Important Than The Course

It's true. Some professors are sent by Satan himself to guard the gates of hell and teach Biology. Avoid these classes by researching your potential professors. Study their class website. Ask former students for their opinions. Check out www.pickaprof.com.

....

43. Save Your Work Every Five Minutes

Computers crash and electricity always cuts out at the most inopportune times. At some point in your college career, you will lose all or part of an important paper. To prevent the total destruction of a potentially brilliant masterpiece, save your computer assignments every five minutes. In addition, email the finished assignment to yourself, and back up your computer files on an external source every month.

....

44. The Laws Of Cramming:

Cramming is inevitable. Just be sure to follow these simple guidelines:

1) Take frequent breaks. Follow every hour-long study session with a true 15-minute break.
2) During this break, avoid all things academic.
3) Hit the sack before a big test. At the very minimum, snag four to five hours of sleep the night before your big exam. Sleep helps your brain organize what you've just learned.
4) If you have a study partner, listen up: The longer you study with someone else, the less productive you both will be. Agree to meet your study partner every two hours for a brief quiz. This can help you examine the material in a new way, and it also breaks up the monotony of a long study session.

....

45. Befriend An Upperclassman

Introduce yourself to an upperclassman that shares your major. They have already survived your course load and can pass along invaluable advice about what professors and classes to avoid. Plus, they just might have old homework and tests lying around. And maybe—if you're lucky—they'll pass along these, too.

....

46. It Is OK Not To Know About Your Future

The minute you start college, everyone will ask, 'What are you majoring in? What do you want to do with your life?' But do not worry if you don't have answers yet. Most 20-somethings do not know what they want to do with the rest of their life. College is about finding yourself, not your career. If you've narrowed down your options by graduation time you've succeeded.

(And while we are on the topic of life after academia, there is no law saying that you have to marry your college sweetheart within a year of graduating.)

....

47. On Plagiarism

Even though plagiarism may save time, some online search engines are designed to spot recycled work, and nothing pisses off a professor more than plagiarism. So be careful. Also: Submitting the same paper in two different classes can be considered plagiarism unless both professors give you the green light to do so. Think hard before slapping your name on something that isn't brand new.

....

48. Take Summer Courses

If you have this option, use it. Summer and evening classes generally involve less time and effort compared to regular semester courses. Also, taking a summer class or two enables you to under load during the school year, which equals more free time for socializing and sports. Avoid overloading at all costs. If you must, stay on campus for an extra semester to avoid overloading your academic schedule.

....

49. Never Partner With Friends

If you need a partner in class and your friend is a dumbass, don't give in to peer pressure. Pair up with someone else. If your friend is smarter than you, you are the dumbass, so don't let him read this book.

....

50. A Five Page Paper Really Only Needs To Be Three Pages

Here are ways to make your paper seem longer:

	Default Page Settings	Altered Page Settings
Font:	Times New Roman	Courier New
Margins:	Left & Right = 0.5"	Left & Right = 0.6"
	Top & Bottom = 0.75"	Top & Bottom = 0.85"
Word Spacing:	0 pt	0.2 pt
Line Spacing:	Single	1.2

On average, English professors are more specific about margins and an exact word count. Make sure that your professor doesn't check for these modifications before lengthening your paper using the above tactics.

....

51. Go To Faculty Office Hours

Instead of asking a question during class, write it down and save it to ask your professor at a later time. Professors love students who visit during faculty hours. This extra effort can pay off—big time—when it comes to determining your grade. Other bonus options are to email your professor questions and introduce yourself to both the professor and the TA's on the first day of class.

....

52. Do Not Cite Wikipedia As A Source. Ever

The word "Wikipedia" may sound like "encyclopedia" but the similarities end there. Wikipedia is an online website with entries that anyone can edit. It is not a scholarly reference. Use it, but make sure to consult a second source, and do not quote or cite it in your final paper.

....

53. GPA's Do Not Really Matter

Here's the deal: GPA's only matter if you plan to go to graduate school. Your first employer only really cares if you have a diploma. After this, it is all about experience.

....

54. Skipping Classes Will Come Back To Haunt You

It's Murphy's Law: 75 percent of the final exam will be based on the chapter of the book that you didn't read. Or, it will cover the only lecture that you skipped. So attend every class (even if you didn't complete that day's assignment).

....

55. Get To Class Early

Arriving late to class means that you'll cause a minor scene and you'll have just a few open seats to choose from. Most likely, you'll wind up sitting at the front of the class—in the professor's full view. Another given? You *will* get called on. To avoid this scenario (and stay on your professor's good side), arrive early.

....

56. Never Schedule A Class Before 9:00 am

If you wake up at 7 am ready to head to class and feeling completely refreshed from a full night's sleep, you are not having enough fun in college. Schedule your classes to begin at 9 am or later. This way, you won't have to worry about heading to bed before midnight.

....

57. Study Abroad

If you have the chance, study abroad.

Your sophomore year is the best time to do this. Why?

1) You should concentrate on making friends during your freshman year.

2) You should concentrate on enjoying your friends during your junior and senior years.

3) In many places around the world, you become an adult at the age 18. During your sophomore year, you are already 18, but not quite an adult by American standards. So, consider studying abroad an excellent chance for you to jumpstart your life as an adult. And remember: Practice makes perfect.

....

58. Obey The Buddy System

In every class, make sure that you have a designated go-to buddy who will take notes for you if you miss class. Choose your buddy wisely, based on handwriting, class attendance record and intelligence (hint: pick a girl).

....

Hygiene & Food 101

"No one likes to hang out with the smelly kid."
- Nick Dyer, Hanover College class of 2006

59. Basic Hygiene Is Essential

1) Brush your teeth everyday and just before you see someone of the opposite sex.

2) Wear lots of deodorant. If you sweat a lot, stick with black or white shirts. If you over apply and get deodorant marks on your shirt, a quick wipe with dry terry cloth (ex: towel, washcloth, robe, etc.) should do the trick.

3) Remember that Febreze does not clean clothes.

4) Always have a secret stash of emergency breath mints and gum.

5) Bring several bath towels; you will use them for everything. (Girls, buy a bath robe. You may think a towel will cover you just fine until your roommate's grandfather and little brother visit unexpectedly.

....

60. Body Wash Can Double As Shampoo

This is especially true for guys. Apply liberally over your entire body. Discard the container if you leave it in the shower over night (or, if you must keep it, apply cautiously. If the "body wash" smells of urine, discard promptly).

....

61. Hot Steamy Showers = Ironing

If your clothes are wrinkled, hang them just beyond the shower and turn on the water full force and super hot. Let the room get steamy (which involves closing the door) and in 10 minutes, the wrinkles will have disappeared. Another laundry tip: Stow a stain removing pen in your book bag or purse for on-the-go treatments—it will save you a lot of scrubbing come laundry time.

....

62. If You Have Stained Underwear, Throw Them Out

Skid marks on your underwear are not okay. To solve this problem, buy only dark underwear and never reuse a pair that isn't clean.`

....

63. Wear Sandals In The Shower

After midnight, college showers become toilets, trashcans, burlesque booths and more. Always wear sandals, and if you drop something on the shower floor, run it through the wash before using it again.

....

64. Do Not Shave Body Parts Unless You Plan to Continue Shaving Them

Got it? Oh, and ladies: Winter is not an excuse to stop shaving your legs. You never know when you might meet the boy of your dreams. And guys: Don't show up to class everyday with a 5 o'clock shadow. Your teacher will appreciate your clean-shaven look. It's a sign of respect.

....

65. Liquor Before Beer

Sipping beer can help you ease out of a drunken stupor whereas downing shots of hard liquor will blast you past the point of no return. When in doubt, remember the rhyme: "Liquor before beer, have no fear. Beer before liquor, never sicker." Also, always remember to eat before a night of drinking, and when you're deciding what to eat keep in mind whatever goes down may come back up. If for some reason you do not have the time to eat, drink a large glass of milk in order to coat your stomach and it will help make for a much friendlier night out on the town.

....

66. Buy White Sheets

You are supposed to change your sheets every two weeks. This will not happen. Darker sheets may mask food stains, but white sheets will hide white stains. People would rather sleep on a food stain than a white stain.

....

67. Even If The Ice Cream Machine Is Free, *Avoid It*

Eating infinite amounts of ice cream will make you fat. So, even though you can have dessert at every meal—pace yourself. Remember: everything in moderation. When you get stressed, try taking a walk instead of self-medicating with a supersized cone. Try to get out, get active and sweat at least 4 days a week. The Freshman 15 is real. Eat a variety of foods and pay attention to portion sizes.

....

68. An Ode To All Things Caffeinated

Caffeine—though you may not know it yet—is a lifesaver. It will help you stay up late at night to cram, and it will also de-fog your brain in the early morning hours when small tasks—walking, eating, talking—seem almost impossible. The good news is, these liquid jump-starts come in many forms (Red Bull, skim lattes, Mountain Dew Code Reds—just to name a few), so find the one that suits your palate best and drink up whenever you need an extra boost.

....

69. Home Cooking = Heaven

In your first days at college, you may not fully appreciate the value of home-cooked food. Then, the cafeteria will serve meatloaf one day and hamburger pie the next. This is no coincidence. Eat every bite of home cooking that you can get.

....

70. Beware Of A Case Of Beer That Costs Less Than $8.00

As good as this may sound, there is a reason the beer is cheap—it tastes like metal. Also, as a general rule, the cheaper the liquor, the more miserable your hangover tomorrow. Try to buy liquor that's been distilled at least four times. And drink light beer. It has fewer carbohydrates. And yes, you need less carbs. Switch now, before it's too late.

....

71. Get Cultured

Match red meat with red wine, and white meats—like chicken and seafood—with white wine. (So, just think "reds with red" and "whites with white.") Also helpful: Learn the difference between a salad and an entree fork. In duplicate utensil settings, the salad fork sits farthest from the plate relative to its forked cohorts. The general rule here is, at the start of a meal, use the outer utensils first and work your way closer to your plate as you dine. And while you won't need to remember these fancy eating rules for soft taco day in the cafeteria, this knowledge will prove invaluable when you first meet the parents of your significant other.

....

72. Drink Lots Of Water

When you are tired or hungry or when more than the usual number of pimples pops up on your skin—ask yourself, "Am I drinking enough water?" If not, you know what to do.

....

Dormitory Life 101

"I don't need to pay a therapist to give me crap. I have a roommate
that does it for free."
-Ally McBeal

73. The True Currency Of College Life: Beer, Milk, And Quarters

These three items are college gold. We mean it. We almost bought a car once for a roll of quarters, two gallons of milk and a pack of light beer. Why are these three items so invaluable? Simple. Cereal is a main dietary staple in college life, and without milk, there is no cereal (just a pathetic bowl of Cocoa Puffs!) As for quarters, anyone who drives and needs to feed a meter or does laundry needs quarters—and they always seem to be in short supply. Last but not least: Beer. College students love beer. We are infatuated by it. It is the forbidden fruit that we can now drink and enjoy to excess. It is, even though this sounds cliché, instant fun and instant cool.

....

74. Lock Your Door When You Leave Your Room

When you leave your room, close and lock your door. When you want to study, close and lock your door. When you are sleeping, close and lock your door. When you want some privacy, close and lock your door. But, keep your door open and unlocked every other chance you get—it's a great way to make friends and signal to others that you're open to socializing.

....

75. Do Not Lend Out Anything That You Are Not Prepared To Lose

Think of anything that you bring to college as community property. Your friends may say (and even truly believe) that they will "bring it back," but don't be surprised if they lose (or sell for beer money) the item in question. If you have something that you cannot possibly stand to lose, leave it at home.

....

76. Make Sure All Your Socks Match And Bring Plenty Of Underwear

The day before you leave for college, throw your socks away. All of them. Then, go out and buy 30 new pairs of socks that match exactly, down to the gold toe thread. Come laundry time, you will thank yourself (and this book) for the move. Speaking of laundry time, socks and underwear are the limiting factors in every wardrobe. Buy lots of these two items to prevent wasting your free time hovering near the washing machines.

....

77. Never Put All The Bills Under Your Name

Even if your roommate is your identical twin brother, do not put all the bills under your name. If you do, you will end up paying for it—literally. An easy way to keep track of utilities and expenses is to create an Excel spreadsheet and review it at the end of each term to determine the exact amount each person owes.

....

78. Ask Permission To Use Other People's Stuff

At some point in your college career, one of your friends will rob you of your last 99-cent frozen pizza. Knowing this, it is perfectly ok to put death warnings on your precious possessions (especially anything edible that you wish to actually eat). If you want to "borrow" from your friends, however, be sure to ask their permission first (this is called leading by example and—surprise!—it really does work).

....

79. Get To Know Your Hall-Mates

Be nice to the weird kid down the hall. He just might let you borrow an extra quarter for laundry, his class notes or the latest Wii game that's impossible to get your hands on. The best part is, he's always headed back to the same place you are, so he's a guaranteed ride home (with someone who won't get lost along the way).

....

80. With Pets, Start Small

If you want a pet, start with a plant. If the plant lives, graduate to a goldfish. If both are alive after two months, it is safe to get a real pet. Do NOT fall in love with the boa constrictor or exotic parakeet in the window. The average dog or cat will set you back $1,500 annually, and when you are out having a good time, the last thing you will want is to bring that "special someone" back to a room full of dog poop. Pets always sound like a great idea. But they deserve all of your attention and love (and you deserve to be irresponsible—that's what college is for).

....

81. Don't Worry About Making Your Bed In The Morning

Making your bed is a losing battle*—you are bound to mess it up again in T minus 24 hours. Besides, you should be spending that precious time doing other, more important things like sleeping, studying or walking someone from the opposite sex to breakfast. You should have your morning routine perfected by the end of your first semester; it should take you a total of four minutes to wake up and walk out the door. If you are running late, it is ok to brush your teeth en route to your final destination. Do not skip this step.

*This rule does not apply during parental visits. Always make your bed when your mother is in town.

....

82. On Duct Tape And WD-40

If it moves and it shouldn't: use Duct tape.

If it doesn't move and it should: use WD40.

If it does both of these, throw it away.

....

83. Power Strips Are A Necessity

Chances are, in your dorm room, you will have just three outlets for your 37 electronic devices. Plan ahead and pack a lot of power strips. But, a word of warning: Linking multiple power strips together in a single outlet is a fire hazard. Do NOT try it. You will not win.

....

Common Sense 101

"Never pass out in a gay bar in your Halloween costume."
- Ben Lye, Hanover College class of 2006

84. Never Go Anywhere Alone

When you are with others, it's not scary; it's a story. Have at least one friend by your side when heading out at night (or when taking off on road trips in search of the perfect chicken nugget).

....

85. Keep Things In Perspective

You aren't the first person in the world to fail a test, walk around for half a day with food stuck to your face or break up with your boyfriend or girlfriend. Life goes on. Things will get better.

....

86. Be Careful What You Download

Much of your college life revolves around your computer, so be careful what links you click and what you upload and download. A video of the world's largest pyramid of midgets may sound cool, but it could wreck havoc on your history paper. Forget it or open it up later—from a friend's computer.

....

87. Whoever Adds A Piece Of Garbage That Causes Two Other Pieces Of Garbage To Fall Out Of The Garbage Can Has to Take The Garbage Out

And don't try to get out of it. Just do it.

....

88. If You Think You've Found An Amazing Parking Spot, You Didn't. What You Actually Found Is A Parking Ticket

Read all the street signs. Scour the sidewalk for fire hydrants. Avoid yellow paint and be sure to stash some loose change in your car.

....

89. Open A Checking And Savings Accounts—At The Same Bank As Your Parents)

You need to do this for several reasons:

1) It will help you learn how to manage your money.

2) It makes it very easy for your parents to "help you out" financially throughout the school year. Be sure to remind your parents of this "coincidence" at the start of every fall semester.

....

90. If You Must Pee In Public. . .

Cops love to write tickets for "indecent exposure," so be sure to have several friends act as lookouts when you're emptying your load in public. Getting hauled into the police precinct is never fun—but it's even worse if you're yanked away still half-full.

....

91. Your Student ID And Room Keys Should Be Held In Higher Regard Than Your Own Life

According to the powers that be at college, both your student ID and your room key are more important and harder to replace than you are. We recommend punching a hole through the corner of your student ID and attaching it to your room key. This set-up makes it super-easy for someone to return your most precious possessions—God forbid you should ever lose them (again).

....

92. Delay Getting A Credit Card

As great as the free T-shirt sounds, it isn't worth it. If possible, wait until your junior or senior year to get a credit card. When you finally feel ready for the responsibility, start slowly. Charge only gas or a small purchase each month and pay the bill via online banking the very next day. Come graduation day, you will have worked your way toward an "excellent" credit rating (and this score DOES matter post-college).

....

93. You Can Always Take Out More College Loans, But You Can't Always Take More College

College loans may seem scary, but they are actually a really smart business deal. Every other loan that you will take out in your adult life will likely have a higher interest rate than your current student loan. This is precisely why investors discourage paying off your student loans early, even if you have the chance. So, just give in to the idea of debt and invest in your education (in the form of yet another $20,000 unsubsidized loan).

....

94. Have A Well-Stocked Medical Kit

You will be surprised at how often this gets used. Make sure to have a thermometer, plenty of Band-Aids, cough drops, Tylenol, Motrin, and both Nyquil and Dayquil.

....

95. Never Leave Your E-mail Account Open When You Leave The Room

If you aren't cautious with your email account, the entire campus just might "mysteriously" receive an e-mail announcing that you have changed your name to "Babyface" or that you are now accepting donations for "gently-used" underwear. So remember: log out!

....

96. You're A Small Fish. Get Used to it

Nothing is more annoying than an undergraduate who thinks he's big stuff. Instead of talking about how great you are and how awesome your high-school was, do the opposite. And girls, just because you're nervous about starting all over in college, don't worry. You will find friends. You will get noticed. Just be patient and don't force it.

....

97. If You Don't Know Already, Learn How To Jump A Car And Fix A Flat Tire

You will get a flat tire or your car battery will die at least once during your college career. When the disaster strikes, impress your friends by handling the situation yourself instead of having to wait four hours for help.

....

98. Save Some Of Your Old E-mails So That You Can Read Them When You Are A Middle-Aged Nobody Stuck In A Boring Job

Trust us.

....

99. Always Have Your Digital Camera Charged And Ready

In college, your friends will document all of the ridiculous things you do so that they can make fun of your stupidity for years to come. Their pictures will also capture some of the best moments of your life. After you leave college, these photos will triple in nostalgic value. Be sure to stow them away in a safe place.

....

100. Always Get The Free Flu Shot

You are going to be living with thousands of people in close quarters. This means that you are going to get sick at some point in the school year. Improve your odds of staying healthy by getting a flu shot in the fall. Yes, shots suck. But it's better than being doubled over on the toilet during exams or—worse yet—during winter break.

....

101. Your Parents Will Read Your MySpace or Facebook Page

If you have a MySpace or a Facebook page, write it as if your parents were huddled over their computers at home, devouring the tidbits on your personal page and feeling like sly little detectives. (And even if your parents don't own a computer, one of their techno-savvy friends could read your page and blab. So watch out.) To further protect your personal life, limit your online "friends" to just your real-life friends. Increasingly, businesses and graduate programs are including MySpace and Facebook pages in their background check. Remember this before posting photos of you in a barely-there, hot pink bustier or passed out on the floor, cuddling a bottle of Jägermeister

....

Extra Credit

Stash these pages where you'll need them most: On the washing machine, in your glove box, on your microwave, etc.

How to Fix a Flat Tire

1) Apply the parking break.

2) Remove the hubcap if you have one so the lugnuts are exposed.

3) Loosen (but do not take off) all lugnuts. To do this turn counter-clockwise (remember lefty-loosy, righty-tighty).

4) Jack the car up (most cars have a notch in the bottom of the car to indicate where the jack should be placed on the frame).

5) Remove the lugnuts, then the wheel.

6) Replace with spare tire.

7) Tighten as much as you can all the lugnuts in a star or criss-cross pattern.

8) Lower the car.

9) Tighten the lugnuts again as much as possible.

10) Replace the hubcap.

How to Jump a Car

1) Try to find a car with the same voltage battery as your own (a.k.a. a car about the same size as yours).

2) Never allow two jumper heads to touch each other or any part of the engine.

3) Attach a red (positive) jumper to the positive battery terminal of the dead car.

4) Attach the other red (positive) jumper to the other cars live battery terminal.

5) Attach a black (negative) jumper to the live cars negative battery terminal.

6) Attach the other black (negative) jumper to any unpainted metal surface in the dead car (preferably as far away from the battery as possible and away from any parts that might move).

7) Let the cars idle for a few minutes. Then attempt to start the dead car. Upon starting continue letting the cars idle for a few minutes until removing the jumpers in reverse order of how you put them on.

What to do if Your Involved in a Car Accident

1) Do not leave the car unless the area is secured. If there are injuries call 9-1-1 immediately. In some states it is against the law to move the vehicle once it's been in an accident. Ask advice from police dispatch if injuries are serious or if you are unsure what to do with the vehicle.

2) If there are no injuries police may not respond but still call the police and report the accident.

3) Turn hazard lights on or light flares to alert other drivers of the accident.

4) Look for witnesses and ask them to stay on the scene. Get their name, address and phone number and copy them down. If you do not have a pen and paper ask to borrow one.

5) Be very careful what you say and write down anything that the other driver says about the accident (i.e. I didn't see you, etc.).

6) Write down the date, time, location (nearest intersection), and weather and road conditions.

7) Copy the information about the other car(s) involved including their make, model, year, license plate number and VIN (located near the driver's-side front window).

8) Ask for the driver(s) license and proof of insurance. Copy their name, address and driver's license number. Also copy the name of their insurance company, the insurance account number, and any customer service number listed on the insurance card.

9) Take pictures of the accident if you have a camera / camera-phone available.

10) If police or medical personnel have arrived at the scene, copy down their information (name and badge number).

11) If your car must be towed, be sure to get the following information from tow truck company: the name, address and phone number of the company, the name of the tow truck driver, the truck's license plate number and their estimated towing fee.

12) Call your insurance company immediately when you return home (after you call your parents).

. . . .

How to Do Laundry

1) Sort your dirty clothes, making separate piles for whites, bright colors and darks. If you mix whites with colors in the wash, the colors may bleed onto and ruin your whites. Also separate clothes that tend to produce lint (towels, sweatshirts, chenille and flannel) from clothes that tend to attract lint (corduroy, velvets and permanent-press clothes).

2) Empty all pockets and close zippers to prevent snags.

3) Pre-treat heavy stains with stain remover following instructions on the product label.

4) Use the cap of the detergent bottle or the cup found in detergent boxes to measure out the right amount of laundry soap. Pour soap into the washer or its detergent dispenser.

5) Choose the water temperature for the wash cycle. In general, use cold water to protect colors and darks from bleeding or fading, and to avoid shrinkage. Use warm or hot water for durable fabrics like cotton (make sure they're preshrunk), and to ensure that your whites stay white. Warm water also helps eliminate germs that can survive through the cold cycle.

6) Start the washer before adding clothes to allow the detergent to dissolve in the water. (very helpful for black light parties). The regular cycle will do for most loads but use the gentle cycle for sheer or delicate fabrics. Adjust the water level to the size of your load.

7) Remove lint from the dryer's lint tray. Put the clothes and a single dryer sheet in the dryer after the wash is complete. Hang delicates (such as bras and certain sweaters) to air dry on a clothing rack or hanger to avoid more shrinkage. Check tags if in doubt.

8) Select the correct drying temperature for your laundry load: low for delicates, medium for most fabrics and high for cotton. When in doubt use low or medium.

9) Once completely dry, remove them from the dryer immediately to avoid wrinkles.

. . . .

How to Tell if a Person is Suffering from Alcohol Poisoning

These general guidelines can help you determine if a person is suffering from alcohol poisoning.

1) If the person is breathing less than 13 times per minute or stops breathing for periods of eight seconds or more.

2) If the person is asleep and you are unable to wake him/her up.

3) If the person is unable to drink any substantial amount (1 cup or more) of water without puking it back up.

4) Look and feel the person's skin. If it is cold, clammy, pale or bluish in color they may be suffering from alcohol poisoning.

5) If the person is continually vomiting (repeated, uncontrolled).

*Keep in mind the person who may have alcohol poisoning has an impaired gag reflex and has alcohol in their stomach which acts as an irritant so puking may occur at any time. With this there's a risk of accidentally inhaling vomit into your lungs, which can lead to a dangerous or fatal interruption of breathing. Excessive vomiting can also result in severe dehydration. Make sure a person who is in danger of this is staying hydrated and is sleeping on their side. Seek medical attention if they exhibit any of these symptoms or you have any doubts.

....

Dinner Etiquette

1) Turn off your cell phone prior to the meal.

2) Do not dominate the conversation by talking more than 50% of the time.

3) Always place your napkin across your lap and use it to wipe your mouth periodically.

4) When unsure of what to order, moderately priced chicken or fish is always a safe bet.

5) Never begin eating before a signal from the host to do so.

6) Your bread is located to your left. Your drink glass is the glass that it located to your right. Be cautious of ordering alcohol. Make sure the situation is appropriate. When in doubt make the "ok" sign with both your hands. Your left hand makes a "b" for bread. Your right hand a "d" for drink.

7) It is not considered good table etiquette to use one's bread for dipping into soups or mopping up sauces. Make sure you tear your bread into small bite-sized pieces.

8) Do not burp, slurp, pick at your teeth, lick your fingers or speak with your mouth full.

9) Do not stretch across someone to reach something. Always ask for the item to be passed to you.

10) Always compliment your host on their selection of food and wine.

11) Once finished the dinner knife and fork go back to the middle of the plate. The napkin goes to the right of the plate.

....

Meals from the Microwave

Spaghetti Dinner:

Ingredients: 1 lb. lean ground beef, 1 onion (chopped), 2 cloves garlic (minced), 28 oz. jar spaghetti sauce, 2 cups water, 1 tsp. dried basil leaves, 8 oz. spaghetti pasta (broken into pieces), 1/2 cup grated Parmesan cheese.

Preparation: In a 3 quart microwave safe casserole, place beef and onions, crumbling beef to break into small pieces. Microwave on high for 3 - 4 minutes, stirring once to break up meat. Microwave on high for 2 more minutes and drain off any fat.

Add spaghetti sauce, water, basil and uncooked spaghetti. Mix gently to combine. Cover with lid and microwave on high for 5 minutes. Stir well. Cover casserole again and microwave on high for 8-10 minutes longer. Stir well.

If you want to freeze this dish, at this point cool the casserole in the refrigerator. Wrap well, label, and attach a freezer bag with the grated Parmesan cheese inside. Freeze up to 3 months. To thaw and reheat, thaw overnight in refrigerator. Cover casserole with microwave safe paper towel and microwave on medium for 7-8 minutes until warm. Sprinkle with cheese and continue as directed below.

If not freezing, sprinkle with cheese, cover again and microwave on high for 7-8 minutes longer until spaghetti is tender. Let stand 4 minutes before serving. 6 servings.

Rice Crispies Treats:

Ingredients: 1/3 cup butter, 1 (10 1/2 oz.) pkg. marshmallows, 1 tsp. vanilla, 6 (1/2 cup) Rice Krispies.
Preparation: Melt butter in bowl in microwave. Stir in marshmallows until melted and smooth. Blend in vanilla. Stir in Rice Krispies. Spread in lightly buttered 9 x 13 inch pan. Cool.

....

Lessons Learned

Following are blank pages that you can fill in what you have learned and pass your own words of wisdom on to those that read this book.

About the Authors

Ben Lye and Nick Dyer are proud graduates from the illustrious Hanover College in Hanover, Indiana and now somehow both hold permanent and very successful jobs with Fortune 500 companies. Ben Lye graduated with 6 disciplinary referrals which included one for falsifying a tornado siren. Nick Dyer still holds the record for a 2+ minute keg stand, most Everclear bonged, and the most parties being kicked out of due to drinking all the beer. They both still maintain the functionality of most of their livers.

The authors of this book can be contacted at:
college101@rocketmail.com

www.ingramcontent.com/pod-product-compliance
Lightning Source LLC
Chambersburg PA
CBHW031321040426
42443CB00005B/171